BRITAIN'S RAIL NETWORK TODAY

ADAM HEAD

First published 2022

Amberley Publishing
The Hill, Stroud
Gloucestershire, GL5 4EP

www.amberley-books.com

Copyright © Adam Head, 2022

The right of Adam Head to be identified as the Author of this work has been asserted in accordance with the Copyrights, Designs and Patents Act 1988.

ISBN 978 1 3981 0616 1 (print)
ISBN 978 1 3981 0617 8 (ebook)

All rights reserved. No part of this book may be reprinted or reproduced or utilised in any form or by any electronic, mechanical or other means, now known or hereafter invented, including photocopying and recording, or in any information storage or retrieval system, without the permission in writing from the Publishers.

British Library Cataloguing in Publication Data.
A catalogue record for this book is available from the British Library.

Origination by Amberley Publishing.
Printed in the UK.

Appointed GPSR EU Representative: Easy Access System Europe Oü, 16879218
Address: Mustamäe tee 50, 10621, Tallinn, Estonia
Contact Details: gpsr.requests@easproject.com, +358 40 500 3575

Introduction

In the 1980s a struggling British Rail released a new slogan for their trains: 'This is the Age of the Train.' At the time of its release the train featured in the adverts was the then-new InterCity 125, or the HST (high-speed train) to give it its alternative name.

The HST's time as the UK's premier train has now passed in favour of newer trains, which is the period this book looks at. This book will be a review of the changes that have been taking place over the country in the past few years.

It features trains from previous years that are still running on the network or have either been transferred to another operator, stored, or, worse, gone for scrap. It will also introduce new operators on the scene who have brought new trains onto the network.

All images taken in this book are my own and were taken within the safety rules and regulations of the railways. Remember, the railways are a dangerous place and can kill if mistreated.

2018

January

A livery that was soon to be partially consigned to the history books was that of ONE blue. No. 170205, seen at Stowmarket, was the last unit to wear it before it was sent to Crewe for an overhaul. There are still a handful of Mk 3 carriages that wear this livery, keeping it from being completely retired.

February

The Class 222 Meridian was built for the Midland Main Line between 2003 and 2005 to replace the Class 170 Turbostars on this line, and to this very day they are still doing just that. All that has changed is the livery and company name; Midland Main Line, became East Midlands Trains in 2007. No. 222007 arrives into Leicester with a service for Nottingham. This Meridian, built as an nine-carriage unit, was shrunk down to five carriages to allow smaller four-carriage Meridians to carry more passengers.

Rail tours are a common sight on the East Coast Main Line; however, seeing them hauled by a Class 67 isn't, which is what we can see here as No. 67008 arrives at Peterborough with a rail tour for Lincoln. These Spanish-built diesel locomotives made by General Motors were originally built to haul mail trains around the UK and replace the older Class 47s, but when the mail contract was discontinued in 2004 their workload dried up. Despite a chequered career on the railways, they have always been able to find work.

In 2018, loco-hauled trains were still very much in operation, and there was no end in sight for these trains running on the Wherry Lines between Norwich and Great Yarmouth/Lowestoft. Using a Class 37 diesel locomotive at either end with three Mk 2 carriages in the middle, it saw a lot of use not only from passengers but enthusiasts too. One of the 37s used was No. 37423 in this unique DRS livery – there is a smaller company logo in the middle and not the usual larger compass logo that takes up most of the body. It is seen at Norwich awaiting departure for Great Yarmouth.

March

All that power for such a small load. DB were increasing the rate that their Class 66s were receiving the new, bright red DB livery, replacing the old EWS livery that they had carried since they were built and shipped over to the UK. The immaculate paintwork on No. 66165 would indicate that this was recently overhauled. It is seen passing through Stoke-on-Trent, heading for Stoke Marcroft engineering yard on the other side of the station.

Great Northern started to provide an increase in services towards London King's Cross. With one service starting from King's Lynn and another from Ely, they were able to provide a half-hourly service into the capital for the rising passenger demand. The stock for these services on weekends were operated with Class 365 Networkers built by ABB at York between 1994 and 1995. In its second decade of work No. 365538 sits on the rear of a service for London King's Cross.

In March 2018, the UK suffered severe weather when 'the Beast from the East' struck and covered the country in snow and ice. Despite these appalling conditions trains still ran as well as they possibly could. On the Ecclesbourne Valley Railway in Derbyshire, they were determined to run trains; unfortunately, they didn't escape the freezing conditions and snow, seen here as No. 33103 arrives into Wirksworth station ready to form a service for Duffield.

April

Unique rail tours take place around the country every weekend, and have done so for many years. They provide unique opportunities to explore rarely used lines such as freight lines, and connect places that aren't commonplace on the modern network. Hastings unit No. 1001 was seen passing through an area that they had never operated. It passes Cambridge with the 'The West Norfolk Wanderer' tour from Hastings, heading towards King's Lynn.

Upgrades to the port at Felixstowe and more rail traffic has resulted in more liner trains. Whereas most of those operated by Freightliner's large fleet of Class 66 diesel locomotives, some of them can be seen in the hands in the much older Class 86 electric locomotives. These are well over fifty years old and are still powering up and down the West Coast and Great Eastern Main Lines. Nos 86614 and 86628 are seen at Colchester heading a train for Trafford Park in Manchester.

There are multiple freight operators in the UK making up part of the modern rail scene, but none are as enthusiastic with liveries as GBRF. They have a small fleet of Class 66s in special liveries that allow them to stand out from the crowd, including BR large logo, London Underground special liveries and this unique BR green livery applied to No. 66779. This same livery was applied to No. 92220 *Evening Star* as it was, like No. 66779, the last of its class to be built. It is seen complete with a British Railways emblem logo and nameplate at Peterborough awaiting a path over to the yard.

Preserved railways such as the Epping Ongar Railway in Essex bring in revenue from families having days out and enthusiasts. They do this by bringing in visitors such as older diesel locomotives like this Class 20, No. D8059, allowing memories of bygone days to be a reality again.

May

A year since its opening and Cambridge North station was going from strength to strength as passenger numbers rose and more train services called at the station. The station serves nearby areas such as the Cambridge Science Park and also has a regular bus service that operates from the city centre. Cambridge North is owned by Greater Anglia and runs regular services to and from London Liverpool Street as well as services for Norwich, which were in the hands of Class 170 Turbostars such as No. 170273, here awaiting departure.

Based at North Walsham, Nenta Traintours run many tours starting in East Anglia and working out towards destinations such as Carlisle, Newcastle and Plymouth. Their choice of rolling stock was always popular with enthusiasts and travellers as they were mainly hauled by Class 47 diesel locomotives, which were at one time commonplace in East Anglia working services between Norwich and Cambridge towards London Liverpool Street. Due to the failure of No. 47746 it became a double-headed tour for Carlisle as the massive train arrives into March heading towards Carlisle.

With multiple units now operating as the main type of train on the network, seeing a loco can be a relief to many. For a long period Norwich was known for being a stabling area for Direct Loco Services (DRS) locos of many different classes. At this time at least four locomotives were seen parked up at Norwich, with Nos 57002, 57007 and 37423 occupying the sidings and No. 37407 hidden behind them and showing off its new BR large logo livery.

June

In April 2017, No. 20227, owned by the Class 20 Locomotive Society, was unveiled in London Underground Metropolitan livery after previously wearing a modern London Underground emblem livery of red, white and blue. However, it wasn't until April 2018 that it was given a new nameplate from London's – if not the world's – most famous sleuth, *Sherlock Holmes*. It was given this nameplate alongside another plaque in the style of a BR shed plate, '221B' – for the apartment the detective lived in. No. 20227 spends its time running back and forth along the North Norfolk Railway and is seen here running around at Sheringham.

The Belmond British Pullman has its place in today's rail scene as it is one of the UK's most luxurious trains, boasting the best of everything while reliving the golden age of train travel. This train usually travels from London on a circular tour, taking in champagne or high tea, or it may travel to places such as Bath or Cambridge, as is the case here. The carriages were built between the 1920s and 1950s and are individually named, some have even carried royalty over the years. This rake of impressive-looking carriages is hauled by a pair of DB Class 67 diesel locomotives (Nos 67021 and 67024), which they acquired in October 2017 and were also painted into the umber and cream colour scheme.

Class 73s plied their trade in the south, working on services between London Victoria and Gatwick Airport and since then they have become a common sight across the country after being acquired by both GBRF and Serco for their Caledonian Sleeper services. These locos are unique for having both a diesel engine and a contact shoe for parts of the country that had a third rail. In 2014, No. 73962 (formerly No. 73204) was unveiled by GBRF after being refurbished at Loughborough with a new MTU engine and new lighting on the exterior, which is visible as it leaves the reception sidings at Ely and breaks new ground with a test train for Derby RTC.

July

Britain's oldest EMU, at forty-two years old and only just holding on to its place in today's railway scene, is the Class 313. These veteran EMUs can be seen on the Southern Region working between Brighton and Seaford, and Hove and Littlehampton, or on the East Coast Main Line working between Welwyn Garden City and Stevenage via the Hertford Loop towards Moorgate. These sets always work in pairs, as seen at Welham Green as No. 313030 leads a Moorgate service. The faded paintwork on the second carriage shows the run-down condition that befell this unit. They were due to be replaced with new Class 717s by Siemens, along with others of their kind, all of which were sadly scrapped on the Great Northern side.

Travelling around Liverpool and its surrounding areas comes courtesy of Merseyrail, who have been operating the area since 1977. They have operated trains such as Class 507s since 1978, replacing the older Class 502 and 503 EMUs. These 40-plus-year-old EMUs are still plying their trade in and around Merseyside alongside Class 508 EMUs too. No. 507027 was seen at Liverpool South Parkway ferrying passengers into Liverpool as the main station, Liverpool Lime Street, was closed for remodelling.

Above and below: The annual DRS open day is a train enthusiast's paradise. The operator opens its door to the public to have a look around either the Carlisle or Crewe depots. In 2018, it was the turn of Crewe depot, which had a selection of multiple different locos on offer to view. In one of the main viewing areas were Nos 57002 (due to be named later in the day), 88002, 68021 and 37424. One of the star attractions was No. 68019 in First Transpennine Express livery in preparation for new loco-hauled services between Scarborough and Liverpool Lime Street.

August

Another of GBRF's special liveried 66s is No. 66718, displaying London Transport livery, which had adorned this locomotive since 2013. It also carries the nameplate *Sir Peter Hendy CBE* after the former commissioner of Transport for London. No. 66718 is seen at March station shunting wagons to and from Whitemoor yard, which can be seen turning off to the right behind the last wagon and the yard just past the station.

A scorching heatwave took hold across the country, so what better way to spend it than going to the seaside. During the summer months Greater Anglia ran a 'Summer Saturday' timetable, offering an increase in non-stop services between Norwich and Great Yarmouth. As they rush to alight the passengers are completely oblivious to No. 37409, in its new BR large logo livery at the helm of the service, waiting in preparation to take the next load back to Norwich.

The Grand Central Railway played host to a number of steam engines at the 50th anniversary of British Railways withdrawing steam engines from the main line in favour of cleaner and quicker diesel locomotives. The heatwave had caused the first attempt of this event to be cancelled due to heat and steam engines not being a good mix where the countryside is concerned. While No. 70013 *Oliver Cromwell* looks on, Nos 48476 and 73069 arrive in Leicester North with a service from Loughborough Central.

September

The imminent arrival of a steam engine is guaranteed to fill station platforms. In September, A4 Pacific No. 60009 *Union of South Africa* slowly builds up speed as it leaves the passing loop at March and heads towards Peterborough, with Chester its destination.

Sadly, not everyone was able to enjoy the experience of being hauled by a steam engine, as seen with No. 47760 passing through Cambridge North trying to regain as much time as possible as it works its train towards Norwich. This was due to A4 Pacific No. 60007 being declared a failure at London King's Cross and No. 47760 being drafted in to haul the train and avoid it being cancelled; It was able to regain a lot of time by not taking its booked water stop at Cambridge.

It's business as usual for LNER's No. 91121 as it arrives into Peterborough with a service for Leeds. These powerful workhorses have been ferrying passengers up and down the ECML since the 1980s and, despite newer trains arriving onto the scene, the end isn't in sight for these yet. However, as more and more Azumas arrived in the coming months the number of active Class 91s has sadly dwindled to a very small amount, the majority having been stored, including No. 91121.

October

Above and below: The year was gradually coming to a close and electrification and the new Class 800s were changing the Great Western scene. A pair of 800s sit at Reading with services for London Paddington and Hereford. Built by Hitachi, the design of these trains is based on the Japanese bullet train. They are designed to hold more passengers and accelerate to their maximum speed quicker than their HST predecessor by using the newly built overhead wires, although they were also fitted with diesel engines should the train be unable to use the overhead wires.

A large number of newer Class 800s were already introduced onto the GWML, but not enough to displace the HSTs, which were still holding on to a lot of diagrams. A work-worn No. 43069 sits at Reading with a service for Bristol Temple Meads, which had yet to be completely taken over by their successors. Since leaving the GWML No. 43069 has since been stored at Long Marston awaiting its fate.

In September 2017, Virgin Trains started to repaint their fleet of Pendolinos into a new livery of what was called 'Flowing Silk', which resulted in an all-over white livery and a flowing red colour on the cab ends. The entire fleet was eventually repainted into this bland livery at the request of the Department for Transport to allow easier transfer of the units should a new franchise holder take over the West Coast Main Line – perhaps they foresaw the future of the WCML. One of the nine-carriage Pendolinos, however, No. 390045 was picked to display the rainbow flag of the LGBTQ community and was also given the hashtag '#ridewithpride', which was well received and also part of a set of many different train operators who had also joined in, such as Great Western Railway and SouthEastern.

November

How does an operator make a 1980s unit look like it belongs in the modern day? By bringing out a demonstrator unit. Greater Anglia unveiled this new look Class 321, with the main differences being different traction motors, air conditioning rather than opening windows and DDA compliance by installing a disabled toilet and a disabled area. This resulted in the Renatus project, which saw Nos 321301–30 receiving upgrades and still operating on the Great Eastern Main Line. However, No. 321448, in its unusual livery, has since been stood down and stored while waiting to be converted into a Class 600, which will run on hydrogen fuel.

The faces of the future at Peterborough. Hitachi's No. 800202, on a test run from York to London King's Cross, meets Siemens No. 700153 with a service for Horsham. These units now form what is quite a common ECML scene between London King's Cross and Peterborough, although No. 800202 is in the much more colourful LNER Azuma livery.

The end of the year is synonymous with a certain train running across the entire country. These trains are called railhead treatment trains (RHTT) and they spray a sandite solution on the rails to remove leaf mulch and improve train reliability and punctuality. In East Anglia they are based at Stowmarket and run towards Clacton, Southend, Norwich and Great Yarmouth, but when a little more maintenance is required they run towards Dereham on the Mid-Norfolk Railway. To access the Mid-Norfolk Railway, however, it requires reversing at Wymondham, which Nos 57301 with 37038 on the rear is in the process of undertaking.

December

Many, many years ago, No. 87002 would have been sat at London Euston. Rather than being stabled it would have been at the helm of a Virgin Trains service most likely headed towards Scotland. While most of the thirty-six have either been scrapped or found a new life in Bulgaria, No. 87002 still flies the flag for the class as the only one operational in the UK. After leaving Virgin Trains, No. 87002 was sold to Serco for their Caledonian Sleeper operations, which mainly involved shunting stock between London Euston and Wembley depot, but has found new life with Locomotive Services Limited after leaving Serco in 2019.

It isn't Christmastime without a steam-hauled rail tour. Seen at Finsbury Park after battling the incline out of London King's Cross is No. 6233 *Duchess of Sutherland*, building up speed while heading towards Lincoln.

A mixture of needing land for the building of HS2 and the curtain starting to come down on the HSTs came to a head when on 8 December the very last HST left Old Oak depot just outside London Paddington. The train was led into the station by No. 43185 with No. 43093 on the rear and was greeted by a large number of train enthusiasts who wished to see a piece of Great Western history. No. 43185 was complete with a headboard commemorating it for being the final HST from the depot.

2019

January

A new year and the end of a decade and Greater Anglia were giving their brand-new trains a test between Norwich and Diss. The first FLIRT to arrive and be tested was No. 755405, as seen in the reception sidings after shunting out of the station for its predecessor, No. 90005, on a London Liverpool Street service. It would be another five months before the first FLIRT would enter service.

PROGRESS to replace these units, which were only supposed to be a temporary stop-gap measure but lasted much longer than everyone's (especially the passengers') expectations. Northern Rail would continue use Class 144s throughout 2019 until replacement with the Class 170 Turbostar and Class 195 Civity. At Sheffield it is business as usual for the Pacers, as No. 144009 awaits departure for Hull and Nos 144011, 142050 and 144005 await their next duties.

By the end of 2020 all twenty-three of the 144 Pacers were placed into storage, with some going to preserved railways the following year. For No. 142050 this would be its last year in service before getting scrapped.

By the start of 2019 there were still defunct liveries still roaming around. Despite Northern undertaking a massive refurbishment program for every train they had acquired from their predecessor, it would appear that No. 158910 hadn't been called up. It is seen at Sheffield in old Northern colours while advertising the Metro line around Leeds, waiting to head back there.

Northern were also in the process of driver training. They had received displaced Turbostars from Scotrail as electrification had seen them replaced with newer EMUs, demonstrating a big improvement over the Pacers they had been brought in to replace. They were very well received and were also refurbished as part of Northern's program. No. 170453 slowly glides through Sheffield, heading to Nottingham.

Newer units were coming onto the Midlands/Yorkshire scene, but the humble Class 150 Sprinter still had its place, even though the earliest examples of these Sprinters were over thirty years old. No. 150214, rests after arriving with a service from Leeds.

The steam engine, once a common sight across the UK, had now been whittled down to a few remaining examples. Here is a 4-6-2 Black 5 built by the London, Midland & Scottish Railway. Of the 842 built only eighteen still survive, one of which is No. 45212, which belongs to the Keighley & Worth Valley Railway in West Yorkshire and was on its way home.

A successful bid from Abellio, the East Japan Railway and Mitsui in 2017 paid off as it got them the West Midlands franchise. Fast-forward two years and the West Midlands went from the uniform colours of lime green on all trains to a mix of light and dark green on the London Northwestern Railway Class 350 Desiros, as seen on No. 360368, and orange for the West Midlands Trains Class 170 Turbostars, displayed on No. 170501, as the franchise was split to work under two names.

The cross-city line between Lichfield and Redditch/Bromsgrove via Birmingham also fell under the West Midlands Trains banner, and that meant another new livery for the Class 323, which had spent their entire lives working this line. No. 323208 departs University with a service for Lichfield Trent Valley via Birmingham New Street.

February

Another train in 2019 that was due for retirement was the Class 315, with at least one unit already being removed from service and scrapped. They could be seen working in and out of London's Liverpool Street with Transport for London and London Overground, who usually passed at Bethnal Green. No. 315809 is heading towards Chingford and No. 315810 back into the capital.

Among the mighty HSTs and IEPs on the Great Western Main Line it is very easy to overlook the smaller operations that still provide a vital service. Heathrow Express was founded in 1998 and pride themselves on making a fast and efficient service between the London termini and the airport with a half-hourly service. The trains used for these services are the Spanish-built Class 332s, of which fourteen were built. The first of the fleet, No. 322001, is seen at London Paddington with another Heathrow Airport service.

The new Class 800s were becoming more and more common on the Great Western Main Line, but the plucky HST refused to give in. Parked next to No. 800010 is No. 43192, which idles before heading for the west. It was to leave the Great Western Main Line but not Great Western Railways as it would become part of the Castle Class HST fleet, which would work between Taunton/Bristol and Cardiff.

Virgin was still in the process of making a fleet of 'Flowing Silk'; however, some Pendolinos were still avoiding the paintbrush as seen here at London Euston with a before and after effect seen on Nos 390131 and 390020 as they wait departure to their destinations.

Snow arrived in certain parts of the UK, but that didn't stop the trains from running as No. 168329 arrives into Oxford with a service from London Marylebone. This is one of nine Class 170 Turbostars that previously worked for First Transpennine before getting transferred to Chiltern Railways between 2015 and 2016 and converted to the large Class 168 Clubman fleet that they operated.

An interesting history lingers around No. 59003. It was built in 1985 for Foster Yeoman but only lasted for a short while. After striking up a deal with DB Cargo in Germany it was modified and sent off to Europe in 1997 working freight trains, which it did for seventeen years before it was taken out of service by Heavy Haul Power International in 2014. In the same year it was sold to GBRF who brought it back to the UK in October and it was repainted into their house colours. The well-travelled loco is seen passing Oxford.

The remains of the previous year's RHTT season are still evident on the Mk 2s as they sit with No. 37425 at Norwich with a short set service for Great Yarmouth.

Sometimes the Greater Anglia Class 90s need to go further afield for maintenance as they need more than Norwich Crown Point are able to provide. No. 90009 had just come back from Crewe, bringing No. 37425, which it shunted into Norwich Crown Point as it was allocated to the short set.

Operating under the cover of darkness while the country sleeps are the track maintenance machines that keep the railways operating. Network Rail's DR79241 is one of their rail grinders. It grinds the railhead to make it smoother for trains to travel across. It is seen here at Cambridge waiting the route out after arriving from the ECML.

March

Looking out over the Huddersfield horizon are a Northern Class 150, a 153 Sprinter and a First Transpennine Express Class 185 Desiro, all waiting time to their various destinations.

On the approach to Eastleigh station is Arriva CrossCountry's Class 221 Super Voyager No. 221128 with a service for Manchester Piccadilly.

It's business as usual for Virgin Trains as both variations of trains that make up their fleet can be seen at Wolverhampton. No. 390151 awaits departure for Glasgow Central while No. 221110 picks up London-bound passengers. It wasn't to make it, however, as it subsequently failed at Sandwell and Dudley and was terminated at Birmingham New Street.

Recently refurbished Class 170 Turbostar No. 170475 sits at Huddersfield with a service for Leeds. At the time of writing these units were temporarily on hire to First Transpennine Express.

Above and below: A pair of unique visitors came to East Anglia in the form of Nos 88003 and 88007, which were brought down to inspect the OHLE on the Great Eastern and West Anglia Main Lines in preparation for the new Stadler FLIRTs that were soon to enter service. A few days later they were hard at work and were seen at Ely leaving the reception sidings as they headed towards King's Lynn.

April

After spending many months being refurbished internally and externally, No. 47635 was unveiled at the Epping Ongar Railway in its immaculate BR large logo livery complete with 'Jimmy Milne' nameplate and Scotty dog emblem from its days based in Scotland. It is seen sitting at Ongar.

At the start of the year DB entered into a new contract with Maritime Transport to haul container trains. At the start of April, DB repainted six of their Class 66s and they were also named 'Maritime Intermodal' followed by a number from 1 to 6. The second 66 of this dedicated fleet is No. 66047, which is seen passing Stowmarket heading a liner train from Wakefield to Felixstowe.

FLIRT testing and training was still underway, and it was common to see at least one of these a day being tested. No. 755410 was being tested between Norwich and Stowmarket on this day and would do a number of these diagrams.

May

A new life awaits three former Great Western Railway Mk 3 HST carriages. Seen at Ely hauled by No. 57303, this convoy is heading to Doncaster where the Mk 3s will be completely refurbished and then sent off to Scotland to work for Scotrail.

To commemorate 100 years of the RAF, Northern unveiled No. 156480 in this spectacular livery complete with a name sticker. It is seen at Leeds shortly after arrival.

Nothing unusual to see here! Well, apart from the train on the left being the wrong way round. No. 82152 waits at the head of the service for London Liverpool Street with No. 90001 on the rear rather than the front.

Above and below: In 2017, Greater Anglia ran their charity-based rail tour called the 'EACH Express 2' and on 18 May they did it again, aptly naming it 'EACH Express 3'. Utilising Nos 37405 and 37409, they took in a lot of the Greater Anglia network. No. 37405 can be seen at King's Lynn, which was a first for the short set as it had never ventured south of Norwich in passenger service before. No. 37409 is later seen at London Liverpool Street after the tour did a complete non-stop run from King's Lynn to the capital via Cambridge and the West Anglia Main Line. Through the generosity between Greater Anglia and the passengers on the tour, a total of £22,000 for the East Anglia Children's Hospice was raised.

June

Another new livery for the 37/4s came in the form of a pre-privatisation InterCity livery, which was applied to No. 37419. Seen at Norwich, it shows off its new livery in the dock siding, but it didn't spend much time in the east as it was moved to Carlisle.

The sight of a HST at Cambridge isn't very common; however, the Network Rail's HST can be seen stabling behind the back of the station between duties from time to time. Painted in all-over yellow, it has been given the nickname of 'The Flying Banana' and is based at Derby when it isn't working across the country checking the conditions of the track and the overhead wires.

Seen passing through Northampton is No. 66780 in its unique Cemex livery after GBRF and Cemex reached an agreement to start moving more aggregate by rail rather than road. The loco picked to carry this livery and the nameplate '*The Cemex Express*' started out life with DB as No. 66008 before being sold to GBRF in 2017, becoming No. 66780.

The Class 319 EMU is another unit that has seen good fortune in the ever-changing UK rail network as they were displaced from Thameslink operations between Bedford and Brighton and around London in 2017. A small number of these units were transferred to London Midland and Northern and the rest went into storage, although 2020 would show these units in a new light.

Above and below: New beginnings in 2019, in two completely different ways. Firstly, No. 92043 is seen passing Bletchley with a rake of brand-new Caledonian Sleeper Mk 5 carriages, built in Spain to replace the old Mk 2 and Mk 3 carriages in operation at the time. Also seen at Bletchley was the Class 230, a converted unit from old D-stock previously used on the London Underground. Rather than going for scrap it is now working the Bedford–Bletchley line for West Midlands Trains. No. 230004 is one of three units built for this line.

July

Advertising '20 years of Direct Rail Services' on what was their 25th anniversary at Carlisle was No. 57307. It is unknown whether this was an advertisement for Direct Rail Services (DRS) as it was the weekend of their open day at Carlisle Kingmoor Depot or if it was the local Thunderbird in case of failure on the West Coast Main Line.

The 2019 DRS open day was held in Carlisle. One of the main attractions of this open day were Nos 37409 and 47593 in BR large logo livery and No. 37419 in InterCity livery, harking back to the days of pre-privatisation. As a result of the DRS open day rail tours were operated to Carlisle, one of which was No. 60163 *Tornado*, which worked with No. 86259 on a rail tour from London King's Cross to Carlisle and a return via Newcastle.

No. 156447 sits at Carlisle with a service for Newcastle. This Class 156 Sprinter and four others were transferred to Northern from Scotrail and still wore the colours of its old operator.

Settled into their new lives, the next chapter of the HST story was in full force at Aberdeen and Penzance. Nos 43030 and 43177, both of which spent their lives working on the Great Western Main Line, were transferred to Scotrail for their Inter7City services, which operate between Glasgow and Edinburgh towards Aberdeen. No. 43177 wears the new livery and No. 43030 still bears the livery of its former operator. No. 43186 sits at Penzance as part of Great Western Railway's Castle Class HST sets, which operate between Cardiff and Bristol towards Taunton, and Plymouth towards Penzance, displacing the Class 150 and 153 Sprinters.

By the start of 2018 the Gospel Oak–Barking line in London was electrified as part of a scheme to increase capacity on this line. The Class 172 Turbostars built for this line were replaced by Class 710 Aventras and therefore transferred to West Midlands Trains. Seen at Leamington Spa, No. 172006 awaits departure for Coventry.

No. 158763 sits at Plymouth with a service for Exeter St Davids. This Class 158 Sprinter had yet to visit the paint shop and still wore the eye-catching local line's livery.

Above and below: Loco-hauled trains can be seen in Wales operating around the Cardiff area for Transport for Wales. A service towards Rhymney was brought in using Class 37s and Mk 2s as a temporary measure due to the older Sprinter units requiring upgrading to meet DDA requirements. One of the 37s used for this diagram was No. 37418 in BR large logo complete with matching Mk 2s seen at Cardiff Central with a Rhymney service. A service that has been around much longer is the one between Holyhead and Cardiff Central, which was advertised as a premier service for workers. Originally operated with Class 57s and Mk 2s, they were replaced with Class 67s and Mk 3s in 2012. No. 67016 sits at the head of the train with a service for Holyhead.

Among the Clubmans, Turbos and Voyagers that operate on the Chiltern main line, it is still possible to see some locos in action between London and Birmingham. Nos 68011 and 68010 meet at Leamington Spa with services for London Marylebone and Birmingham Moor Street. These are two of the six Class 68 locos that Chiltern Railways operate.

Another new acquisition for the Caledonian Sleeper was six Class 73/9s, which were to be used to operate the sections from Aberdeen, Fort William and Inverness to Edinburgh Waverley where the entire train was taken to London using a Class 92. Seen at Aberdeen awaiting time is No. 73986 with its portion of the sleeper heading to Edinburgh Waverley.

Class 91s – three different ones. A range of different colours fill the platforms at London King's Cross, awaiting their journeys up the East Coast Main Line: No. 91111 in its commemorative First World War livery; No. 91132 in former Virgin East Coast Trains livery, now LNER red with 'Employer Pledge' advertising; and No. 91119 in InterCity livery.

August

Above and below: Usually seen in passenger service, it is unusual to see them operating without the rest of their train, as seen with No. 91101 heading to Doncaster and No. 90005 heading to Crewe for an exam.

Above and below: A before and after in South London as London Overground were repainting their entire fleet of Class 378 Capitalstars to look like the new Aventras they were operating. No. 378223 wears the original scheme while No. 378136 is wearing the new colours.

To commemorate 100 years of the end of the First World War in 2018, Great Western Railway unveiled No. 800306 in this special livery that names everyone from the Western Region who gave their lives during the war – the names cover the entire length of this train.

With time running gradually running out, the LNER HSTs still hold onto work on the ECML. No. 43317 is seen passing Huntingdon with a service known as 'The Northern Lights' heading north to Aberdeen.

Is it 2019 or 1989? Nos 37419, 37402 and 37424 are seen all wearing colours of the past at Norwich.

From the Great Western Main Line to the Great Eastern Main Line via the North London Line. Class 345 Aventra No. 345005 sits in Acton yard behind Rail Operations Group Class 37 No. 37608 requiring attention. In time these units will be seen working Crossrail between Shenfield and Reading.

It's not unheard of for a train to break down while in service, however inconvenient it may be. Seen at Sandy, DB Class 67 No. 67005 is heading towards Bounds Green depot in London with a failed LNER set in tow.

No. 47579 at Mangapps Farm Railway in Essex is a sight reminiscent of days gone by. A time when BR blue and named trains were a common sight at places like London Liverpool Street, where Class 47s and 302s regularly worked.

Flying Scotsman has a massive fanbase across the UK rail network, with both old and new flocking to see it when it moves about. It is seen here heading towards Southall in London, passing Huntingdon and working down the East Coast Main Line from York.

September

Freightliner Class 66 No. 66413 sits in Ipswich yard showing off its new black and orange colour scheme.

Freight around the Southern Region isn't as frequent as other areas, but it doesn't stop Class 66s turning up as a large yard at Tonbridge station is regularly used to stable locos when not being used. In its new eye-catching Newell & Wright Transport livery is No. 66747, heading to the yard with No. 66701, which wears a special variation of GBRF's very first livery for their 66s.

Passing through Attleborough station is DB Class 66 No. 66041 providing the traction for a Branch Line Society rail tour that originated at Nottingham and finished at Norwich. It wasn't plain sailing for this tour, however, as there was a pair of DB Class 66s on it, but No. 66088 had failed at Brandon and had to be removed, thus making this very late.

To increase capacity on the Fife Circle during the peak hours, Abellio Scotrail ran two loco-hauled services using hired-in Class 68s and Mk 2 carriages from DRS. Seen at Dalmeny with a mix and match rake of carriages is No. 68006 with a service for Glenrothes with Thornton.

No. 43131 leads an Inter7City HST service into Edinburgh Haymarket with a service from Aberdeen.

Above and below: The Class 170 Turbostar has been plying its trade around Scotrail since the turn of the millennium; however, the all-over blue livery of No. 170416 can't hide the fact it will soon be pastures new for this unit as the new Abellio-owned East Midlands franchise will take delivery of these units. One of the main reasons it will be leaving Scotland is the electrification of the Edinburgh–Glasgow route in 2017 and their replacement in the form of the Hitachi Class 385, which took over these duties.

In their final year of work, No. 314216 is seen at Glasgow Central with a Cathcart Circle service. A small number of these units gained the newer Scotrail Saltire livery, whereas the rest stayed in the old SPT livery. As part of the new future laid out for Scotland's railways the entire fleet of Class 314s, bar one (No. 314209), were scrapped.

Seen in and around the Edinburgh area is No. 334004. Multiple units such as these make up a large majority of the UK rail network.

Fitting right in on their home territory, Nos 73136 and 73109 depart the yard at Tonbridge with a circular test run.

Since Govia took over the Thameslink franchise in 2014, one of the trains most synonymous of the London and Bedfordshire areas is the Siemens Class 700, which run between Bedford, Gatwick Airport and Brighton. Two examples of this class, Nos 700015 and 700041, are seen at West Hampstead Thameslink.

Arriving into Ipswich is No. 90001. This loco had recently made history on the Great Eastern Main Line as Abellio Greater Anglia unveiled the new Norwich in 90 service. As part of a franchise agreement a service had to travel between Norwich and London, with a stop at Ipswich, within 90 minutes; this service can easily achieve this target.

A loco with a very uncertain future, one that nearly had scrap on the cards, is No. 50017. It is seen resting in its new home on the Great Central Railway. In the BR era there would have been a higher chance of No. 50017 being obtained by another region, but as franchises operate units for many different reasons the only option for older locos is preservation.

D1705 (No. 47117) has spent many years on the Great Central Railway. A former Class 48, it is the only one of its class left as the other four of the fleet were scrapped. It is seen shunting at Loughborough Central.

November

In 2019, the Class 313s had racked up an impressive forty-three years in service. A majority of the fleet were retired and scrapped earlier in the year as Great Northern had them replaced with newer trains from Siemens. However, Southern continue to run these old trains on services out of Brighton towards Hove and Seaford, proving that not all trains on the UK network need to be the latest and greatest to provide a service.

The changing faces of the Yorkshire train services: a Class 185 Desiro meets a Mk 5 driving trailer at York with services for Manchester Airport and Scarborough. The rake of Mk 5 carriages on the right were built and introduced to release the 185s from those services as they suffered from overcrowding.

Above and below: During the transition from East Midlands Trains to East Midlands Railway a small number of their fleet were still going through a minor refurbishment scheme and therefore the livery was changed, adding another variation to the UK rail network. These changes can be seen with Nos 158773 and 156414.

Above and below: The East Midlands Region of the UK network is one area that is served by a variety of different units from different operators. Seen at Leicester is No. 170113, one of Arriva CrossCountry's large fleet of Turbostars that operate in both directions from Leicester. Currently stabled, it will later work to Birmingham. Seen 27 miles down the line at Nottingham, Nos 153357 and 153358 are seen arriving into the station.

Above and below: Picking up work where they can, DRS used their fleet of Class 37/4s to provide the power for the East Anglia RHTT circuits. Arriving into Colchester after coming off the Clacton-on-Sea line are Nos 37403 and 37424, which will reverse here and head back towards Stowmarket where they are based. In the East Midlands it is the same story but with different traction, as DB Class 66 Nos 66143 and 66101 arrive in Leicester yard.

DB Class 66 No. 66100, proudly showing off its poppy and '*Armistice 100*' nameplate, passes through Stratford with a rake of empty wagons for Acton.

November 2019 saw the ten former DB Class 66s that had been sold back in December 2017 in operation on a multitude of different services. The former No. 66046, now No. 66782, is seen passing through Stratford with a train filled with containers for Birmingham.

Devoid of all branding and living on borrowed time before a new life in Wales, No. 170208 is seen at Stowmarket with a service for Ipswich. Shortly after this image was taken it was removed from service, alongside No. 170201, and transferred to its new depot in Cardiff.

December

Above and below: The sun was setting on No. 170271 and the career of the Class 170 Turbostar on the Greater Anglia network. After starting operations in 1999 and 2002, it was finally the end. No. 170271 was the last of the twelve-strong fleet left in the area. Arriving into Bury St Edmunds, it forms a service for Ipswich; however, the Turbostars were already settling into their new lives in Wales as No. 170273 sits at Cardiff Central with a service for Ebbw Vale Town.

Harking back to the old BR days, No. 313201 was repainted into its old blue and grey livery while it was getting refurbished to celebrate the heritage of the train. This unit has become part of the national collection and will be preserved in the National Railway Museum for future generations to enjoy.

It was the final year for many trains that had spent many years in operation. Two of these trains were the Class 315s and 317s, such as Nos 315806 and 317729. Both were seen at their home of London Liverpool Street for many years. The Class 315s and 317s were bowing out to different variations of the new Bombardier-built Aventras.

The Pacers were to be removed from service by the end of 2019 in accordance with the DDA compliance laws that were due to be put in place in January 2020. However, a delay in new rolling stock allowed trains such as No. 143624 an extended period of running, with the last of the Class 143s being retired in 2021.

A newly named No. 43170 arrives into Cardiff Central after arriving with a service from Taunton.

Wearing its First World War commemoration vinyls is No. 395018, seen at Ramsgate station with a service for Margate. Southeastern operate twenty-nine of these out of London St Pancras towards the Kent coast.

Resting between driver training duties is No. 66749, heading back to Peterborough after a trip to London King's Cross.

December can only mean one thing – it's nearly Christmas. This is a big opportunity for both passengers and train enthusiasts as it means a variety of different tours operating across the entirety of the network. No. 47802 sits at the helm of a rail tour at London King's Cross heading to Lincoln for the popular Christmas market.

The Christmas rush to get away before the seasonal engineering works started had struck again on the East Coast Main Line as No. 91113 arrives at Peterborough with a busy service for Edinburgh Waverley.

The year ended with one last highlight. After spending multiple days operating the LNER's 'Let's Go Round Again' rail tour to give the HSTs on the ECML a well-deserved final farewell, No. 43006 (formerly No. 43206) leads the HST stock, which was completely repainted into its old BR blue and grey livery through March as it heads to Ely for long-term storage.

2020

Due to the coronavirus pandemic and subsequent lockdowns some months of 2020 have been omitted.

January

The Class 442 is another long-distance EMU that has been ferrying passengers on the lines out of London Waterloo since the late 1980s. No. 442408 sits at Portsmouth Harbour with a semi-fast service for London Waterloo. Sadly, 2020 was to be the last year that the 442s would see passenger service before being withdrawn.

Above and below: January 2020 saw the continuation of seasonal engineering works on the East Coast Main Line and therefore meant diversions for the services. Trains were diverted from the ECML at Peterborough and were going via Ely and Cambridge before connecting back onto the ECML at Hitchin. First Hull Trains Class 180 Adelante No. 180111 passes through Whittlesea while LNER Class 800 Azuma No. 800105 is seen passing March.

February

Above and below: A line that is often overlooked is the Chiltern Main Line running between London Marylebone and Birmingham. It is often seen as a competitor to the West Coast Main Line. Banbury sits 70 miles north of London and sees a variety of passenger and freight trains. DRS Class 68 No. 68008, on hire to Chiltern Railways, rests at Banbury before heading towards London and DB Class 66 No. 66107 powers away after a crew change.

An acquisition from Grand Central back in 2018 was the addition of three HST sets comprising of six carriages, which allowed extra capacity for passengers on the Midland Main Line. Seen in de-branded East Midlands Trains livery, No. 43480 arrives into Bedford with a service for Nottingham. These too would see withdrawal by the end of the year.

March

Arriva CrossCountry Class 43 HST No. 43366 arrives into Sheffield with its rake of next generation Mk 3 carriage to ensure their continued use with a service for Plymouth.

Resting between duties on the Caledonian Sleeper is GBRF Class 92 No. 92020 at Edinburgh Waverley. This will remain here until it is required in the evening.

Complete with its British Transport Police advertising livery across the entire length of the train is Class 170 Turbostar No. 170407, which sits at Glasgow Queen Street shortly after arriving.

Above and below: Hitachi hits the ECML. Both First Hull Trains and Transpennine Express show off their new trains in their different liveries as No. 802303 departs Doncaster and No. 802203 arrives into York.

July

Above and below: After being released from the first coronavirus lockdown, the passengers of the Eastern Region were starting to get a glimpse of the future as both the GEML and WAML were now running the new Class 745 FLIRTs full time, with their predecessors being removed from service. On the GEML Nos 745004 and 745006 meet at Ipswich, and on the WAML Nos 745108 and 745103 meet at London Liverpool Street.

London Overground's Class 710 Aventras were slowly introduced into service during lockdown to operate on the Lea Valley lines to and from London Liverpool Street. No. 710123, with its increased capacity and new features such as air-conditioning and USB plug sockets, arrives into London Liverpool Street next to No. 315805.

Above and below: C2C, like many operators, were now running larger trains to meet the requirements for social distancing despite the passenger numbers being at an all-time low. No. 357032 sits at Shoeburyness with a service for London, and No. 357323 arrives into Upminster with a service for Shoeburyness.

August

Network Rail's mobile maintenance train, DR97806, is seen at Benfleet. These types of trains usually operate during the night.

One-off liveries can be found all over the UK rail network. No. 387105 was given this treatment as the unit originally worked for Thameslink and Great Northern before transferring to Gatwick Airport while their fleet were out for maintenance; therefore it gained the Gatwick Express logo, which caused confusion when seen at places like Ely.

Still holding on to what little work it has left, No. 315839 sits at Shenfield with a service for London Liverpool Street.

Forming a service for Manchester Piccadilly is Arriva CrossCountry Class 221 Super Voyager No. 221126 at Basingstoke. The Voyagers form long-distance services from Bournemouth towards Manchester, going via places such as Reading and Birmingham.

Extra capacity has never been too much of an issue on the South Western Railway network, even more so when they took delivery of all twenty-four Class 456s from Southern. No. 456005 leads a stopping service to Woking with two Class 455s in tow.

The large yard at Clapham Junction sees a lot of use during the weekends. South Western Railway are seen taking full advantage of the space.

No. 168111 departs Oxford and is one of many trains across the UK rail network that received 'Thank You NHS' branding for their continued work throughout the coronavirus pandemic.

Oxford sees a small number of freight trains through the station. Colas Rail Class 70 No. 70807 is one of few that will pass throughout the day.

Passing through Clapham Junction, No. 37025 trails on the rear of a test train as it negotiates the points towards Kensington Olympia.

September

Nos 60100 and 60024 pass through Nottingham. A large number of these locos were built but only a small number remain, with a lot being stored at the nearby yard at Toton.

There is still no end in sight despite living on borrowed time, as No. 143601 sits at Barry Island.

A new acquisition for Transport for Wales and once again utilising old trains for a new purpose is Class 769 No. 769003, seen departing Cardiff on a driver training run. This was originally No. 319003 and was built for the Thameslink network, where it spent its entire life before being converted in 2019.

New stations on the UK rail network aren't commonplace for multiple reasons, but Abellio Greater Anglia opened the new Meridian Water station on the West Anglia Main Line in June 2019. Located between Cheshunt and Tottenham Hale, it is serving a new housing estate area that was being built there. Class 379 Electrostar No. 379022 sits at Meridian Water with a service for Stratford.

October

By the end of 2019 the Class 710 invasion had been completed as Nos 710125 and 710121 rest between duties.

The future brings new designs of trains that could once only be dreamt of. With better lighting, the mandatory requirement for a yellow front is no longer required. Class 717 Desiro No. 717005 arrives into Finsbury Park with a service for Moorgate.

No. 08484 is seen hauling No. 745104 from Norwich station to Norwich Crown Point depot. No. 08484 is one of two Class 08 pilots that can be seen occasionally working in the depot or the station. The oldest of this class was built in 1952, with them still proving very versatile after fifty years of use.

Colas Rail took a number of Class 37s that had been previously been working on preserved railways and brought them back to their former glory on the main line again. No. 37099 was one such example. It was based at the Gloucester Warwickshire Railway until it left in 2016 and went to work for Colas Rail where it is seen working mainly test trains such as this one at Peterborough.

Unveiled in August 2020, No. 390119 *Progress* shows off its new livery as it passes Stafford with a service for Liverpool Lime Street. This colourful livery, which covers the entire eleven carriages of this Pendolino, was designed to represent the LGBTQ community around the world.

Above and below: The end of 2019 was to be the end for the venerable Class 483s, which had been operating on the Isle of Wight Railway since removal from the London Underground network at the end of the 1980s. Due to the age of these trains the majority of them had unfortunately been withdrawn; in fact, only two were left in service – Nos 483008 and 483006. However, both of these wouldn't make it to the end of the year after separate failures on both units would see them withdrawn.

Nestled in the heart of the Isle of Wight is a small, preserved steam railway running at just over 5 miles. It could arguably be known as the UK rail network's most southerly preserved railway. On the approach to Haven Street is one of many steam engines based on this railway – Hunslet Austerity WD198.

November

Providing the traction for the yearly RHTT trains in East Anglia were these Class 66s, as Nos 66428 and 66426 head towards Shenfield.

November 2020 saw the introduction of Class 720 Aventras on test for Abellio Greater Anglia. Built by Bombardier and part of the large Aventra family seen around the UK, they were first tested on the Southend line to replace the older Class 321s that had been operating on that line for many years. No. 720536 arrives into Rayleigh with a test run to Shenfield.

December

December 2020 saw the country hit by a large snowstorm, but this didn't prevent No. 720537 from being tested as part of Abellio Greater Anglia's testing program for the Aventras on the Great Eastern Main Line.

Another member of the 'Thank You NHS' decorated fleet of trains was No. 717011, which was branded by Great Northern. It is seen at Welwyn Garden City with a service from Moorgate.

Northern Class 170 Turbostar No. 170454 sits at York with a service for Leeds via Harrogate.

No. 950001 sits in Welwyn Garden City's yard, which sees very little use. No. 950001 is a specialist track recording DMU built in York for Network Rail as part their vast number of different trains used for inspecting track and infrastructure. It uses the same bodyshell as the Class 150 DMU. It will remain in the yard until used for track inspection during the night.

2021

April

April 2021 saw the withdrawal the HST on the Midland Main Line. After previously finishing on the Great Western Main Line and East Coast Main Line, this was the last main line for them to be seen operating regularly on. East Midlands Railway was determined not to let this moment pass without a proper send off and therefore repainted No. 43302 into InterCity livery and No. 43274 into East Midlands Railway colours and ran a regular service on the MML before their final withdrawal in May of the same year.